CONTENTS

FOREWORD

The game of Mah-Jong has been played in Britain since the early part of the twentieth century. It was spectacularly popular in the 1920s and is now enjoying a resurgence.

Those who have played Mah-Jong before will understand and appreciate its enduring qualities: the beauty of the materials, the excitement of the play, the fascination of the style and the formality of its Eastern tradition.

Over the years, although the basic precepts of the game remained the same, various alterations and additions to the rules made playing outside one's usual circle difficult and contentious, as Mah-Jong appeared to have as many dialects as Chinese. Beginners found themselves lost in a welter of irrelevant and confusing practices, which detracted from the essential pleasure of the game. It was time to call a halt to the uncontrolled proliferation of 'home rules' and establish an authoritative yet familiar code of play.

As a consequence, the British Mah-Jong Association was founded, and its first action was to ask Gwyn Headley and Yvonne Seeley to compile a standard set of rules. This reassessment and essential clarification of the game of Mah-Jong still stands for all players as the definitive rulebook.

The co-authors, both Mah-Jong players of skill and imagination, have imparted their enthusiasm in this book, together with their own knowledge and experience. Their contribution has undoubtedly led to a wider appreciation of the game.

D. W. Seeley
President,
British Mah-Jong Association

Mah-Jong was developed around 1850 from Chinese card and domino games.

INTRODUCTION

Mah-Jong is a compelling, easily learned table game for four people, played with a set of 144 pieces called 'tiles'. The aim of the game is to collect four sets of tiles, three sets made up of three or four identical tiles, plus a pair.

COLLECTING TILES

Tiles are collected either by picking up from the 'pack' or a discarded tile, and then throwing out one tile every turn. The winner is the first to lay out a completed hand. This is called 'going Mah-Jong'.

BMJA RULES

Until the British Mah-Jong Association (BMJA) was established, the game's rules were a jumble of different approaches that were confusing to beginners.

In writing this book, we have clarified the basic points and presented a simple yet comprehensive set of rules. We have followed traditional methods of play as closely as possible, although some additions to the original game made on its introduction to the West in the 1920s have been retained, as we believe they improve its quality and excitement.

Nonetheless, the BMJA rules are a distillation of the way Mah-Jong has been played for over 90 years. You will find no newly invented rules here. *Know The Game: Mah-Jong* tightens up existing standards of play, provides an authoritative and workable set of regulations, and provokes a new and lively interest in the game. Serious players in most Western countries now accept the BMJA rules in this book as the standard for the game. Enjoy yourself!

THE HISTORY OF MAH-JONG

Surprisingly, Mah-Jong is among the most recent of the world's major table games. Unlike chess, Go, dominoes, backgammon or draughts, Mah-Jong in its present form can only be traced back to the end of the nineteenth century.

ORIGINS

When it was first introduced into the Western world in the early 1920s, a great selling point was the game's antiquity, its origins being shrouded in the mists of time. Most evidence, however, points to the game being developed in the Ningpo area of China in the 1870s, and most manuals on the game published in the 1920s confirm this.

Many rummy players can master the basic practices of Mah-Jong in a very short time once the terminology has been learnt.

ARRIVAL IN THE WEST

Although there are records of British Mah-Jong players in China before the First World War, the game did not reach the West until it was launched in the United States in the early 1920s. With astute promotion, it became a craze and, like all crazes, it died after a few years.

Mah-Jong tiles use colourful and intricate designs. This is the 1 Bamboo tile.

MAH-JONG TODAY

In its present form, Mah-Jong is most closely linked to rummy. The basic premise of picking up a card or tile to complete a set of three is common to both games.

The complexities of the advanced game require skill, insight, and knowledge. This is why, over the duration of a whole game, which can last up to five hours, the more experienced players will inevitably win.

NATIONAL DIFFERENCES

Several different games can be played with the standard Mah-Jong set. The basic game as it has evolved in China, Japan, Australasia, the United States and Britain has taken on differing national characteristics so there can never be one definitive way to play. Seen through Western eyes, the Chinese game appears a fast, noisy, stylised form of rummy for high stakes, whereas to Easterners, the Western game seems slow, unnecessarily complicated and of little interest to gamblers.

CHINESE DOMINOES

Joseph Babcock, who popularised Mah-Jong in the West, claimed to have developed it himself. Its origins, in fact, seem to be based partly on Chinese forms of dominoes and a card game called '108 Brigands', popular since the seventeenth century.

 This tile is the flower tile belonging to East Wind.

THE MAH-JONG SET

Mah-Jong may not be as cerebral as chess, as easy as backgammon or as chancy as poker, but no other game uses such beautiful equipment. Mah-Jong is played with engraved and painted pieces, plain on the reverse and decorated on the face, along with two dice and, in the West, wooden racks.

THE TILES

The playing pieces for the game of Mah-Jong are known as 'tiles', and there are 144 tiles in a set. Traditionally, they are made of ivory or bone dovetailed into bamboo, although in cheaper sets they will be made of plastic. The characters of the various suits are engraved on to the white face of the tiles in red, green, blue and black. The size of the tiles varies from set to set, but average 30 x 20 x 15mm.

THE SUITS

There are three suits: Bamboos, Circles and Characters. Each suit consists of 36 tiles numbered 1 to 9 inclusive, with four tiles for each number.

In the Bamboos suit, numbers 2 to 9 show the relevant number of bamboo sticks. The number 1 Bamboo is usually represented by a bird, or occasionally by a bamboo shoot that resembles a pineapple.

Beginners should be careful not to confuse this tile with the Flowers and Seasons, which will be discussed later. The 2s, 3s, 4s, 6s and 8s of Bamboo are coloured green, and the 1s, 5s, 7s and 9s both red and green. The importance of the green tiles will be seen later.

The tiles in the Circles suit are marked with coloured discs from 1 to 9. The tiles in the Characters suit are marked with the Chinese numerals from 10,000 to 90,000. The relevant Arabic numeral is also usually marked on the top left-hand corner of each tile.

> The quality of the set adds immeasurably to the pleasure of the game. Always buy the best set that you can afford.

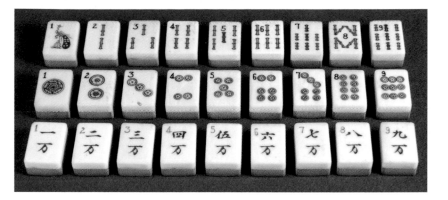

The three suits: from top to bottom, Bamboos, Circles, Characters.

BUYER BEWARE

Many sets are offered for sale on the Internet, but beware. While looking beautiful and being presented in elegant boxes or cabinets, most of these are oriental sets and the tiles lack the Arabic numerals and Roman letters to aid identification.

Different types of the 1 Bamboo tile.

9

THE WINDS

There are four Wind tiles: East, South, West and North. Each Wind is represented both by the Chinese ideograph and by the Roman letter E, S, W or N. There are four pieces for each Wind, making 16 tiles in all.

THE DRAGONS

There are three Dragon tiles: Red, Green and White. These are easily recognised by colour, although the White Dragon, normally a blank tile, may sometimes be outlined in red or blue. Again, there are four pieces for each Dragon.

THE FLOWERS AND SEASONS

Although having no part in the actual play, these eight tiles are valuable as bonus points. They constitute the major element of chance in the game. When one is picked up in the course of the game, it is immediately displayed face up on the table and replaced in the player's hand by a loose tile from the top of the 'kong box' (see page 20).

The Flowers and Seasons are the most attractive and ornate pieces. The four Flowers, numbered in green from 1 to 4, are engraved with a stylised plum blossom, orchid, chrysanthemum and

▲ The four Wind tiles.

▶ Different types of the White Dragon tile.

◀ The three Dragon tiles.

bamboo. The four Seasons, numbered in red, denote Spring, Summer, Autumn and Winter, although the engravings on them follow no recognisable pattern, varying enormously from set to set.

The Flowers and Seasons tiles marked with the number 1 belong to the player who is East Wind, number 2 to South Wind, number 3 to West Wind and number 4 to North Wind. Any player picking up their own Flower or Season during the game will double their score once the round is over.

ENGRAVER'S ART

In the finer Mah-Jong sets, the engravings on the Flowers and Seasons tiles represent the very best of the engraver's art.

 The four Flower tiles.

 The four Season tiles.

PLAIN TILES AND JOKERS

In many sets there are four spare plain tiles to be used if any piece is lost, when one can be engraved and coloured as a replacement. It is always advisable to alternate the use of White Dragons (see page 10) with these tiles so that they wear and age with the rest of the set, otherwise the newly engraved replacement pieces will be obvious to all.

In some sets there are four joker tiles, often marked with a Chinese horse or decorated with colourful plants and artefacts plus a Chinese ideograph for 'joker'. These are used to replace the 2s of Bamboo in the playing of a 'goulash' (see page 26). When no jokers are included, the 2s of Bamboo may be used instead as 'wild' pieces.

DICE

Two small dice are included in the set. These are rolled at the beginning of the game to determine who breaks the wall and where (see page 18). Traditionally, the Chinese dice have the 1 and 4 coloured red, with the other numerals in black.

TALLIES

Since Mah-Jong is primarily a gambling game, there are usually a number of scoring tallies in the set. There are four varieties of tally in the complete Mah-Jong set. The number of dots on each tally does not necessarily correspond to the value of that tally. In a gambling game of Mah-Jong, each player starts the game with tallies to the value of 2,000 points.

The four plain tiles.

Different types of joker tiles.

WIND DISCS

As well as Wind tiles, higher quality Mah-Jong sets also include Wind discs. These are small counters engraved with the Chinese ideographs for North, South, East and West. They differ from the Wind tiles by not having the additional Roman letters E, S, W and N. The Wind discs are used to determine who is to be each Wind for the first hand instead of the Wind tiles (see page 16).

VALUES OF TALLIES

At the beginning of the game each player is given the following.

- 2 x 500 point tallies
  = 1,000 points
- 9 x 100 point tallies
  = 900 points
- 8 x 10 point tallies
  = 80 points
- 10 x 2 point tallies
  = 20 points

  Total = 2,000 points

Dice, tallies and Wind discs.

If a non-gambling game is played, use a pencil and paper to record the score after each round.

13

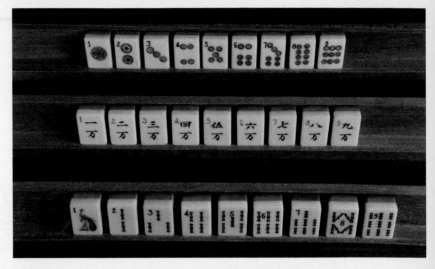

RACKS

To facilitate play, long wooden racks are used to hold each player's tiles. These are not usually supplied with the set, but may be bought separately. One of these racks is coloured black and is used by the person who is East Wind. As East passes from player to player, so does the black rack.

The three suits on racks.

MATERIALS AND ENGRAVINGS

Prices of Mah-Jong sets vary enormously. At the top end of the market, and very rare, are the ivory and bamboo sets, each tile hand-engraved and painted in anything up to eight colours. They are arranged in trays in beautiful mahogany, rosewood or Chinese lacquer cabinets. At the bottom come the machine-moulded and stamped plastic tiles, in tin or wooden boxes, or the slivers of reconstituted wood pulp with garish two-colour transfers.

HANDS IN CHINA

Chinese players scorn the use of racks, preferring to hold the pieces on the table or in their hands, like experienced domino players.

Try to buy the best set you can afford. A craftsman's set is far more enjoyable to play with.

MAH-JONG SETS

Mah-Jong sets can be made from:
- Bakelite
- bamboo
- bone with bamboo back
- cardboard
- Catalin (a type of American Bakelite, with butterscotch coloured tiles)
- ivory
- metal, including silver
- plastic
- wood

MAH-JONG CARDS

Much cheaper but much rarer than tile sets are Mah-Jong cards. These consist of 144 cards representing the Mah-Jong tiles. The game is played as normal, but with the cards being dealt from a standard pack as opposed to a wall (see page 18).

Mah-Jong cards.

PRELIMINARIES

At the beginning of the game, assemble the tiles, dice, racks and tallies on a square table, with four chairs for the players. If a gambling game is to be played, put tallies to the value of 2,000 points in front of each player's chair.

CHOOSING THE WINDS AND SEATING POSITIONS

Take one of each of the four Wind tiles, or Wind discs if included, place them face down on the table and shuffle them. Each of the four players then picks one tile (or disc) and puts them face up on the table in front of them. The player who picks East Wind is the leader for the first round. The player who picks West Wind sits opposite the East Wind. The player who picks South Wind sits to the right of the East Wind, while the player who picks North Wind tile sits to the left of the East Wind. Note that these positions are not the standard points of the compass. The East Wind player not only starts the game, but also scores double and pays double to all the other players.

STARTING PLAY

Once the Wind positions have been established and the players are seated, all the tiles, excluding the jokers and the four spare tiles, are placed face down on the table. Two players (usually South and North, but never East) then 'wash' (shuffle) the tiles thoroughly. This is known as the 'twittering of the sparrows', named after the characteristic sparrows' song. When the East Wind player judges the tiles to have been 'washed' sufficiently, he or she calls 'Pow!'.

ORIGINS OF THE NAME

The name of Mah-Jong is probably derived from the shuffling noise at the beginning of each game, since Mah-Jong in Chinese literally means 'the game of the sparrows'.

 Mah-Jong tiles stored in trays.

TONG BOX

Once the Wind positions have been ascertained, the Wind discs can be placed in a small box known as a Tong box or Chuang-tzu, with the East disc on top to show the prevailing Wind, or 'Wind of the round' (see page 28). If the Wind tiles are used, they are replaced face down on the table to be included in play.

 The four Wind discs and two dice.

BUILDING THE WALL

Each player takes 36 tiles and, keeping them face down, builds a wall in front of him or her. The wall should be 18 tiles long and two tiles high. The four walls are then pushed together to form a square, which symbolises the Great Wall of China.

The walls must touch in the corners to prevent the dragons or evil spirits of Chinese legend entering.

The player picked to break the wall then throws the two dice again. He or she adds the total of this throw and the previous throw together, and counts along the wall in front of him or her, from right to left. The player breaks the wall where the count ends. So, if East throws a 3, West will take the dice and throw again. If West throws a 5, making a total of 8, he or she will count along the wall from right to left until the eighth pair of tiles is reached. The player removes these tiles and places the top one on the fourth pair of tiles from the right and the bottom on the sixth pair. They are called 'loose tiles'.

If the total of the two dice throws adds up to 19 or more, the count continues round to the wall of the player to the left where the break is made and the deal started.

BREAKING THE WALL

The East Wind player throws the two dice to determine who breaks the wall. Counting anticlockwise and starting with him or herself as number 1, the number of the dice will indicate who is to make the break. So the South Wind player breaks if a 2, 6 or 10 is thrown, West if a 3, 7 or 11 is thrown, North if a 4, 8 or 12 is thrown, and East if a 5 or 9 is thrown.

SETTING THE LIMIT

Before the game starts, a limit should be agreed for the most points a player may score in one hand. This is generally 1,000.

The wall (East Wind is nearest the camera).

Breaking the wall.

THE DEAL

Starting from the break in the wall, the next four tiles (two pairs) to the left of the break are dealt to the East Wind player, the next four to South, four to West, four to North and so on, until each player has 12 tiles. Then the first and third tiles on the top row of the dealing end of the wall are dealt to East, the first on the bottom row to South, and the next two to West and North respectively. Now each player takes his 13 tiles (except East who has 14) and arranges them in the rack in front of them.

If any Flowers or Seasons are dealt into a player's hand, they must be declared immediately by putting them face up on the table in front of the player and replacing them with the appropriate number of loose tiles from the kong box (see below). The East Wind player takes the replacement tiles first, followed by the other players in anticlockwise order.

> Tiles are dealt clockwise to each player, four at a time. This is the only clockwise action in the game.

THE KONG BOX

The final seven pairs of tiles at the end of the wall, including the two loose tiles on top (14 tiles in all), are detached slightly from the rest of the wall. This is known as the 'kong box' (see photo below), and its function is to provide replacement tiles for Flowers, Seasons, or kongs (see page 24). If no one goes Mah-Jong, the hand ends when the last tile before the kong box has been played.

DIRECTION OF PLAY

Like many rituals and routines the reason for the predominantly anti-clockwise direction of play is not documented, nor is the change in direction for the deal – that's just the way it is.

 Ready to deal. The kong box is shown at the upper left.

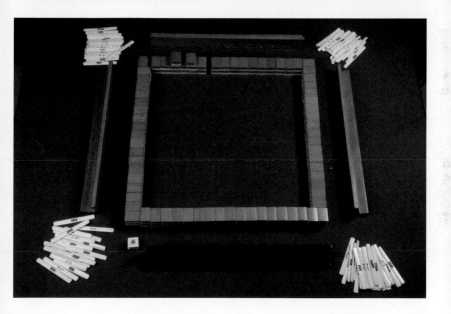

 The kong box comprises 14 tiles.

THE GAME

The basic aim of the game is simple: it is to collect four sets of three or four identical tiles, plus a pair. On achieving this the player calls 'Mah-Jong'. The sets of tiles are known as 'pungs', 'kongs' and 'chows'.

 Close-up of a pung.

 Close-up of a kong.

 Close-up of a chow.

A PUNG

A 'pung' is a set of three identical tiles, for example three 4 Bamboos, three Red Dragons, three West Winds, or three 9 Circles. If displayed on the table they are described as 'exposed'; if held in the hand they are 'concealed' and are worth double (see page 32).

A KONG

A 'kong' is a set of four identical tiles, for example four 6 Circles or four East Winds. As with the pung, a concealed kong is worth double an exposed one.

A CHOW

A 'chow' is a run of three tiles in the same suit, for example 5, 6, 7 Circles; 1, 2, 3 Bamboos; or 7, 8, 9 Characters. Here again the chow can be concealed or exposed, but as it is a non-scoring combination and is only used to enable players to go Mah-Jong, it makes no difference. There can be no chows of Winds or Dragons since they are not numbered tiles.

PLAY – THE FIRST MOVE

Play begins when the East Wind player discards one of his or her tiles, placing it face up inside what remains of the wall and declaring its name at the same time, for example '2 Circles'. Any other player holding two or three tiles identical to this discard may, if they wish, call 'Pung' or 'Kong', take up the discarded tile and place it face up with the two or three from their hand on the table in front of them. They then discard a tile in the same manner as the East Wind player, and play continues. Remember, in Mah-Jong, play proceeds in an anticlockwise direction. Any player coming between the one who discards and the one who picks up that discard misses their turn until play reaches them again.

If no one picks up East's discard, the player on his or her right, i.e. South, may take the tile to form a chow. So if East throws out a 1 Character, and South holds a 2 and a 3 Character, South may call 'Chow' and place the discard and his or her own tiles on the table in front. South then discards a tile and play moves on.

EXPOSED AND CONCEALED

When a pung or chow is claimed from a discard, it is placed face up in front of the player; when a kong is claimed the tiles are placed three face up and one – usually at one end of the set – face down. Once someone has gone Mah-Jong, concealed pungs are displayed with the centre tile face down. Concealed kongs are shown with both end tiles face down. Chows are always face up.

PLAY CONTINUES

From East's first discard, play moves anticlockwise, with each player in turn picking up a tile from the open end of the wall (where the dealing ended), putting it in their rack and then discarding. This routine is only interrupted when a player pungs, kongs or chows.

The standard Mah-Jong hand permits only one chow per player.

DECLARING A KONG

When a player declares a kong (see page 22), whether collected in their hand from the wall (concealed), or made from a discard (exposed), he or she must put the tiles on the table in the form explained earlier (see page 23) and pick one replacement tile from the loose tiles on the kong box (see page 20). The player places this tile in his or her hand and discards a tile as before. Only players with three identical tiles in their hand may declare a kong from a discard. Anyone with an exposed pung must pick a tile from the wall to make their set of three identical tiles into a kong. Whenever a kong is made, either from a discard or from the wall, one tile must always be taken from the kong box.

CALLING OR FISHING

Once a player reaches the stage where they need only one more tile to complete their hand, they are said to be 'fishing' or 'calling', and their hand is a 'calling hand'. They must declare that they are 'one for Mah-Jong'. This declaration serves as a warning to the other three players, who must think carefully before making a discard.

PRECEDENCE

If during the course of the game two players want the same tile, the player closest to the right of the discarder has precedence if both need the tile for a similar purpose, but a player going Mah-Jong has precedence over a player requiring a pung, and a pung has precedence over a chow.

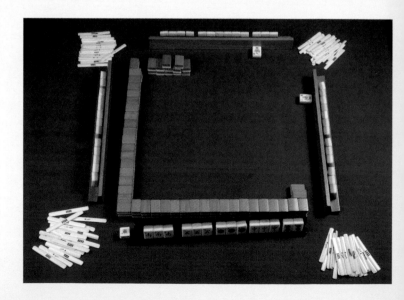

North going Mah-Jong by picking up the 4 Bamboo.

When a player has declared they are 'one for Mah-Jong', any thoughtless discard could give away the game.

SIMPLE ETIQUETTE

- Think of others and don't hold up play by dithering – make quick pickups and discards.
- Work out a basic strategy for each hand and try to stick to it.
- Don't make false claims – other players will get annoyed.
- Listen to and remember what's been discarded.

Deal completed, with replacement tiles taken from the kong box.

ROBBING THE KONG

If a player is fishing or calling for Mah-Jong (see page 24), he or she may find that another player has a pung of the tile needed exposed on the table in front of him. If that player then picks a tile from the wall and declares a kong, the player who is calling for Mah-Jong may claim the tile, thereby 'robbing the kong'. This doubles the score of the player going Mah-Jong.

Robbing the kong is not such a coup as it may at first appear because, apart from special hands (see pages 38–49), the only set that can be completed by robbing a kong is a chow, which scores nothing, and also forfeits a double for no chows in the winning hand. Therefore robbing the kong merely enables a player to go out in an otherwise hopeless situation.

If no player is able to go Mah-Jong, play ends when the last tile from the wall is picked, excluding any tiles left in the kong box. The game is called a 'wash-out' and the 'goulash' comes into operation (see opposite).

THE GOULASH

If included in the set, use the four jokers to replace the four 2 Bamboo tiles. If there are no jokers in the set, the 2 Bamboo tiles are said to be 'wild', and may replace any other tile.

The preliminaries for a goulash are identical to those for a standard game (see pages 16–17): the Wind positions are chosen using the Wind tiles or discs, the tiles are placed face down and shuffled, and each player builds a wall in front of them. The wall is broken, and changes only occur once the tiles have been dealt out.

Having looked at their hand, each player picks three tiles that they

MAKE THE MOST OF A GOULASH

The opportunity to exchange three tiles three times – and to be able to look at each set of three before deciding what to exchange next time – should pay dividends. Try to identify the possibility of collecting a special hand or concentrating on just one suit.

would like to exchange and places them face down in front of them. Tiles are then exchanged three times: first with the player opposite, then once with the players on either side, as follows:

1. East with West, North with South

2. East with South, West with North

3. East with North, West with South.

Between each exchange, players look at the tiles, deciding which to keep before exchanging again. After all the exchanges are completed, play continues as normal with the East Wind player discarding a tile (see page 23). The only difference is that no chows (see page 22) are allowed in a goulash, unless they are part of a special hand (see pages 38–49).

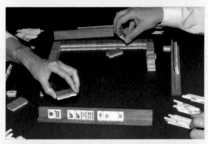

 Exchanging tiles in the goulash.

 The four jokers.

In America, a goulash is called a charleston.

THE PREVAILING WIND

At the start of the game, the East Wind is the 'prevailing Wind' or 'Wind of the round'. If the East Wind player goes Mah-Jong, he or she retains the position for the next game. As soon as any other player goes Mah-Jong, the East Wind (and the other winds with it) moves on one player to the right. So South Wind becomes East and takes the black rack, West becomes South, North becomes West, and East becomes North.

When each player has been East Wind once, the first round is over and the prevailing Wind for the next round is South. The prevailing Wind player always scores double and pays double to all the other players.

A complete session of Mah-Jong finishes when all four Winds have been the prevailing wind and each player has been East Wind four times. As this can take up to four hours, it is fine to end a game at any mutually agreed time.

MINOR, MAJOR AND HONOUR TILES

The suit tiles numbered from 2 to 8 are classed as minor tiles; 1s, 9s, Winds and Dragons are classed as major tiles. Majors are generally worth double the value of minors. In addition, Winds and Dragons are also known as 'honour' tiles and have the potential of earning double scores, unlike the 1s and 9s.

 Minor tiles (The suit tiles numbered from 2 to 8 are classed as minor tiles).

 Major tiles (1s, 9s, Winds and Dragons are classed as majors).

BOUQUETS

Players who pick up their own Flower or Season can double their score once. If they hold a full set or 'bouquet' (1 to 4) of Flowers or Seasons (but not a combination of the two), they are allowed to double their score twice. So, a player lucky enough to hold a set of Seasons from 1 to 4 and his own Flower, is entitled to double his or her score three times.

ORIGINAL CALL

On rare occasions, players may find after their first discard that they hold a calling hand (see page 24), where they need only one more tile to complete their hand. They can declare this as an 'original call'. As long as they make no changes to their hand until they pick up a tile from a discard or from the wall with which they can go Mah-Jong, they are allowed to double their score an extra time.

When a goulash comes into play (see page 26), the Wind positions remain as they were for the previous hand.

DEAD TILES

Discarded tiles that are not immediately punged, konged or chowed are known as 'dead' tiles and take no further part in the game.

A Bouquet.

GOING MAH-JONG

To go Mah-Jong, a player must have four sets of three or four tiles plus a pair. The player must also have declared that he or she is 'one for Mah-Jong'.

CONDITIONS FOR DECLARING MAH-JONG

Apart from the special hands (see pages 38–49), there are certain conditions that players must fulfil before they can declare Mah-Jong:

- their hand must consist of a minimum of 14 tiles, including four sets and a pair

- the four sets can be pungs and/or kongs, and one chow

- there must always be one pair of identical tiles, and only one chow is permitted

- Flowers and Seasons are not included in the minimum of 14, they are bonus tiles.

It is not essential for all the sets to be of the same suit, although many players frown on 'dirty' hands, as well as hands including a chow. However, when a player is dealt a really poor hand with little prospect of improvement, 'going out dirty' is good defensive play and usually the only way of averting a heavy loss.

In every case, including all special hands, a player must declare that he or she is fishing or calling before going Mah-Jong (see page 24). He or she must then wait until a later turn to collect the required tile before going out.

Count up scores quietly and make sure others have completed the task before declaring the total.

Players should try to vary the kind of hands they collect - otherwise opponents will soon catch on and amend their discard strategy accordingly.

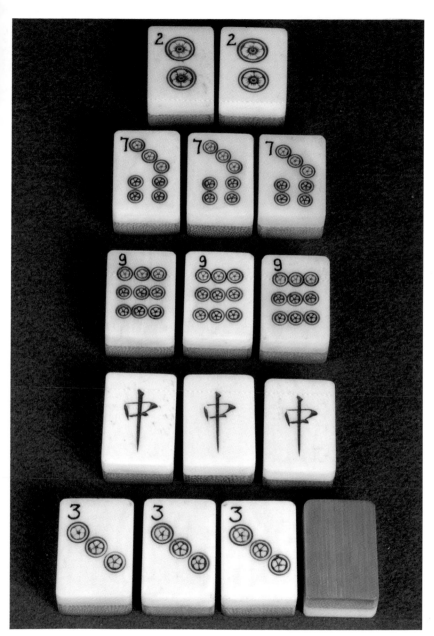

Going Mah-Jong, minimum of 14 tiles, 4 sets and a pair.

SCORING

As soon as one player goes Mah-Jong, all the players display their hands in order to count up their points. The scoring of the basic hands is straightforward, but the bonus scores and the doubling need careful attention. The only departure from this system of scoring is for the 'special hands', which are detailed on pages 38-43.

BASIC SCORING UNITS

The basic scoring units are the pungs and kongs (see page 22). Concealed pungs and kongs are worth double the exposed ones. The scores can be calculated using the chart below.

	Points
Exposed pung of minor tiles (2 to 8)	2
Concealed pung of minor tiles	4
Exposed pung of major tiles (1s, 9s, Winds and Dragons)	4
Concealed pung of major tiles	8
Exposed kong of minor tiles	8
Concealed kong of minor tiles	16
Exposed kong of major tiles	16
Concealed kong of major tiles	32
Chow (exposed or concealed)	0

BONUS POINTS

In addition to these standard scores, there are a number of special bonus points which apply to all players:

	Points
Pair of player's own Wind	2
Pair of the Wind of the round	2
Pair of any Dragon	2
Each Flower or Season	4

GOING MAH-JONG BONUS POINTS

For the player who goes Mah-Jong, there are even more bonus points:

	Points
For going Mah-Jong	20
For drawing winning tile from wall	2

DOUBLING

If players hold certain tiles, or combinations of tiles, they may double their base score. The two score charts below show the doubles that apply to all players and those that only apply to players who go Mah-Jong.

Doubles for all players

	Doubles
Pung or kong of own Wind	1
Pung or kong of the Wind of the round	1
Pung or kong of any Dragon	1
Holding own Flower	1
Holding own Season	1
Original call (fishing)	1
Holding complete set of Flowers	2
Holding complete set of Seasons	2

Doubles for players who go mah-jong

	Doubles
No chows	1
All concealed hand of different suits with Winds and/or Dragons	1
All one suit with Winds and/or Dragons	1
All 1s and 9s with Winds and/or Dragons	1
Going Mah-Jong with a loose tile	1
Going Mah-Jong with last available tile from wall	1
Going Mah-Jong with final discard	1
Going Mah-Jong by robbing the kong	1
Going Mah-Jong from an original call	1

SCORE LIMITS

As it is theoretically possible to score phenomenal amounts, players usually fix a limit above which no player can score. In a tournament, the limit is 1,000 points and this is recommended for all play.

Try to memorise the combinations of tiles that double your base score.

SETTLING UP

There are two points to remember when settling up: every player, no matter what his or her score, pays the player who goes Mah-Jong, and East Wind always pays and receives double. A simple example is as follows:

- **South** Wind goes Mah-Jong with a score of 80 points. West has 60, North has 40 and East has 20. In settling up, West and North each pay South 80 points, but East will pay him or her 160 points. North pays West 20 points, the difference between their scores. East pays West 80 and pays North 40, double the difference between the scores. So after the round, South wins 320 points, West wins 20, North loses 60 and East loses 280.

EXAMPLE OF A COMPLETED HAND

- The limit is 1,000 points; South is the prevailing Wind; West has gone Mah-Jong.

- **East** had a calling hand and was waiting for the 8 Characters or 9 Bamboo to go Mah-Jong with a special hand called 'Triple knitting' (see page 39). Since East had a calling hand, he or she receives one fifth of the limit, i.e. 200 points (see the score for 'Triple knitting').

- **South** needed another pung and a pair before he or she could go Mah-Jong. South's hand is scored as follows:

	Points
Exposed pung of 1 Circles (major tiles)	**4**
Concealed kong of 2 Circles (minor tiles)	**16**
Exposed kong of 5 Circles (minor tiles)	**8**
Pair of Red Dragons	**2**
White Dragon, Green Dragon	**0**
Basic score, no doubles	**30**

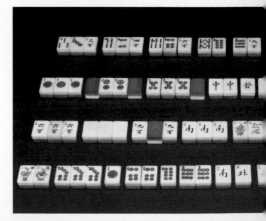

Example of four completed hands.

West went Mah-Jong. This player's hand is scored as follows:

	Points
Exposed pung of 6 Characters (minor tiles)	2
Exposed pung of White Dragons (honour tiles)	4
Concealed pung of 9 Characters (major tiles)	8
Exposed pung of South Winds (honour tiles)	4
Pair of Red Dragons	2
Own Flower (3)	4
Season	4
For drawing winning tile from wall	2
For going Mah-Jong	20
Basic score	50
Plus doubles	
Pung of Wind of the round	**1 double**
Pung of White Dragons	**1 double**
Holding own Flower	**1 double**
No chows	**1 double**
All one suit with Winds and Dragons	**1 double**
Basic score doubled five times	1600
Limit is 1,000 points	1,000

North either played very badly or had shocking luck. North's score is as follows:

	Points
Two Flowers	8
Exposed pung of 7 Circles (minor tiles)	2
Pair of 6 Circles, pair of 9 Circles, pair of East Winds, 1 Circles, 8 Circles, North Wind, South Wind	0
Basic score, no doubles	10

Settling up: North and South each pay West 1,000 points, East pays West 2,000 points. South pays East the difference between their scores doubled, i.e. 340 points, and North pays East 380 points. North pays South 20 points. Therefore, at the end of the round, West wins 4,000 points, East loses 1,280 points, South loses 1,320 points and North loses 1,400 points.

> **Remember that it's perfectly feasible – and quicker – to note scores with pen and paper, and not worry about tallies or payments.**

COMPLETED HAND: EXAMPLE 2

The limit is 1,000 points; East is the prevailing Wind; North has gone Mah-Jong.

East had five unpaired tiles and was therefore some way from completing his or her hand, which is scored as follows:

	Points
Concealed kong of 7 Bamboo (minor tiles)	16
Pung of East Winds (honour tiles)	4
Chow of 2, 3, 4 Bamboo	0
8 Bamboo, 9 Bamboo, North Wind, West Wind	0
Own Flower (1)	4
Season (2)	4
Basic score	28
Pung of Wind of the round (East)	1 double
Pung of own Wind (East)	1 double
Holding own Flower	1 double
Basic score doubled three times	224

South had three pairs to complete before going Mah-Jong, so South's score is as follows:

	Points
Concealed kong of 1 Characters (major tiles)	32
Pair of 4 Characters	0
Pair of 6 Characters	0
Pung of Green Dragons (honour tiles)	4
South Wind	0
Pair of Red Dragons	2
Flower (4)	4
Season (4)	4
Basic score	46
Pung of Dragons	**1 double**
Basic score doubled once	92

 Example of four more completed hands.

West had a calling hand and was waiting for a South Wind tile to go Mah-Jong with 'The wriggling snake', a special hand (see page 42). Since West had a calling hand, he or she receives two-fifths of the limit, i.e. 400 points. West also holds two bonus tiles, i.e. Seasons 1 and 3. Normally the Season 3 would double West's total score, but this is not applicable to special hands. It can only double his or her bonuses.

	Points
Two Seasons (1 & 3)	8
Holding own Season	1 double
Bonus scores 16 points, added to basic calling score	416

North went Mah-Jong. North's hand is scored as follows:

	Points
Exposed kong of 6 Bamboo (minor tiles)	8
Exposed pung of 1 Bamboo (minor tiles)	4
Exposed pung of 8 Bamboo (minor tiles)	2
Exposed pung of 4 Bamboo (minor tiles)	2
Pair of South Winds (neither Wind of the round nor player's own)	0
Flower	4
For going Mah-Jong	20
Basic score	40
No chows	1 double
All one suit with Winds and Dragons	1 double
Basic score doubled twice	160

Settling up: the player who goes Mah-Jong may not necessarily have the highest score. However he or she cannot lose because every player has to pay him or her no matter what the individual score may be. South and West each pay North 160 points. East pays North double, i.e. 320 points. South pays West 324 points (416 - 92). East pays West 384 points (416 - 224, doubled). South pays East 264 points (224 - 92, doubled). Therefore at the end of the round, North wins 640 points, East loses 440 points, South loses 748 points and West wins 548 points.

SPECIAL HANDS

Special hands are sets of 14 tiles, generally collected
in the hand (i.e. concealed), which are harder to create
than the standard four pungs and a pair. The extra effort
is worthwhile as the scores for special hands can be
significantly higher.

RECOGNISED COMBINATIONS

There has been more controversy
over what can or cannot be classed
as a special hand than any other
aspect of the game. The purists
insist that any hand not in use by
the early 1920s contravenes the
philosophical spirit of the game,
while other players invent unlikely
combinations with improbable
names and incredible scoring
powers. The BMJA recognises
the following 19 special hands.

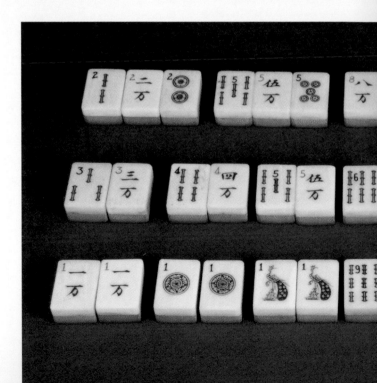

Each description also includes the score when the hand is successfully achieved and the player is able to go Mah-Jong as well as the score available if the player is calling and another goes Mah-Jong. The limit is set at the beginning of the session - generally 1,000 - so a half limit score is 500, two-fifths of the limit is 400 and one-fifth is 200.

Triple knitting

- Half limit
- Four sets of three tiles in the different suits and a pair: no Winds or Dragons
- Calling: one-fifth of the limit.

Knitting

- Half limit
- Seven pairs of tiles in any two out of the three suits; no Winds or Dragons
- Calling: one-fifth of the limit.

All pair honours

- Half limit
- Seven pairs of 1s/9s/Winds/Dragons
- Calling: one-fifth of the limit.

From top to bottom: Triple knitting, Knitting, All pair honours

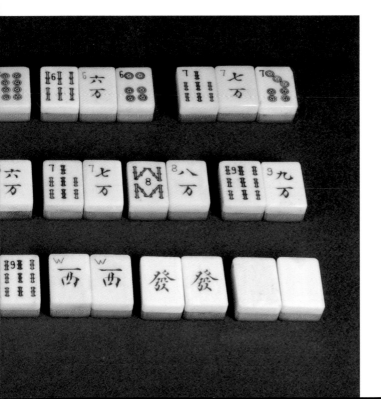

Buried treasure

- Limit
- Concealed pungs in one suit with Winds/Dragons and a pair
- Calling: two-fifths of the limit.

Fourfold plenty

- Limit
- Four kongs and a pair
- Calling: two-fifths of the limit
- Suits may be mixed.

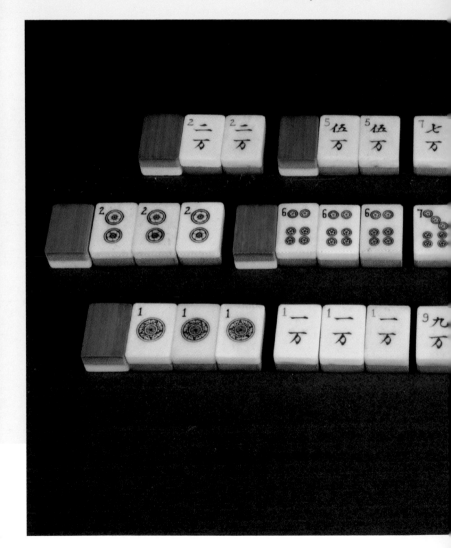

Heads and tails

- Limit
- Pungs/kongs/pair of 1s and 9s
- Calling: two-fifths of the limit.

 From top to bottom: Buried treasure, Fourfold plenty, Heads and tails.

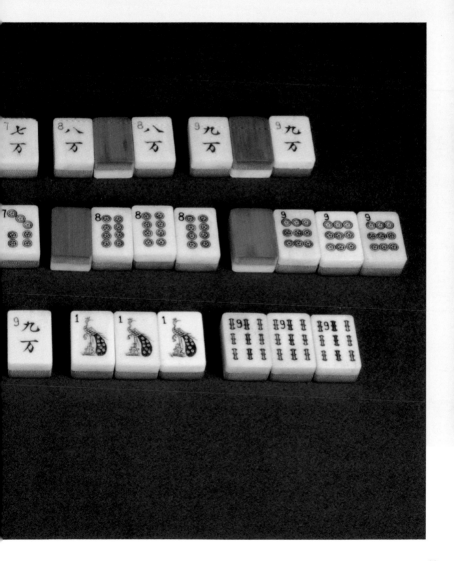

The gates of heaven

- Limit
- A concealed pung of 1s, a concealed pung of 9s, a run from 2 to 8 with one pair, all in the same suit
- Calling: two-fifths of the limit.

The wriggling snake

- Limit
- A pair of 1s and a run from 2 to 9 in the same suit (ideally Circles, because the pair of 1s represent the eyes of the snake), with each of the Winds
- Calling: two-fifths of the limit.

Purity

- Double three times
- Pungs/kongs of any one suit and a pair. No Winds, Dragons or chows
- Calling: double three times.

 From top to bottom: The gates of heaven, The wriggling snake, Purity.

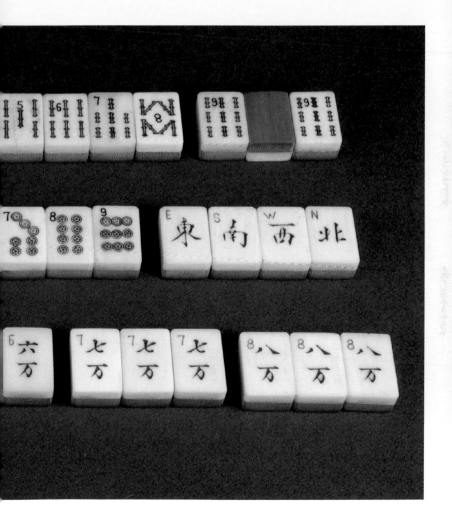

All Winds and Dragons

- Limit.

- Pungs/kongs of Winds/Dragons; no suit tiles

- Calling: two-fifths of the limit, or intrinsic value (whichever is the greater).

> **Collecting a Special Hand is tricky, but the rewards are great.**

▼ From top to bottom: All Winds and Dragons, Imperial jade, The 13 unique wonders.

Imperial jade

- Limit

- Pungs/kongs of the green tiles, and a pair. Green Dragons and 2s, 3s, 4s, 6s and 8s of Bamboo are the green tiles

- Calling: two-fifths of the limit.

The 13 unique wonders

- Limit

- One of each Dragon, one of each Wind, one of each 1 and one of each 9. Any of these tiles must be paired, preferably the 1 Circle.

- Calling: two-fifths of the limit.

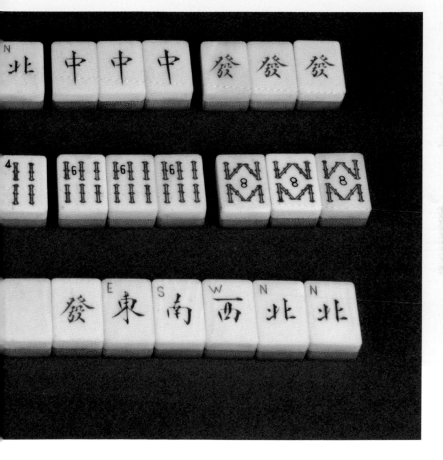

Three great scholars

- Limit
- Pungs/kongs of all three Dragons, another pung/kong and a pair
- Calling: two-fifths of the limit, or intrinsic value (whichever is the greater).

Four blessings hovering over the door

- Limit
- Pungs/kongs of each of the four Winds, with any pair
- Calling: two-fifths of the limit, or intrinsic value (whichever is the greater).

 Three great scholars, Four blessings hovering over the door.

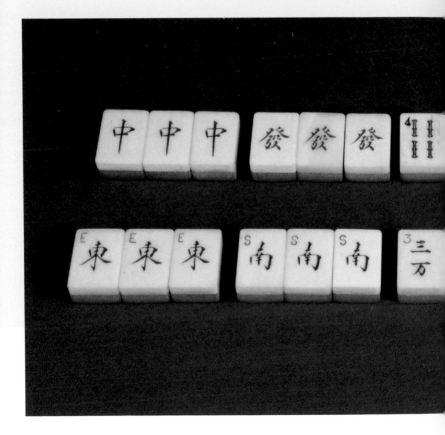

POPULAR HANDS

Experience shows that The 13 unique wonders is the most popular special hand to attempt, closely followed by The wriggling snake and Purity. Neither is easy and the most frequently achieved are Knitting or Triple knitting.

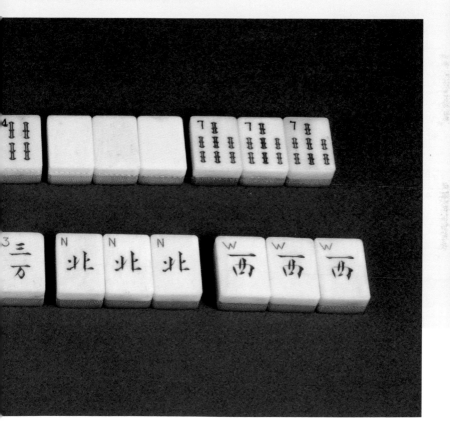

Earth's blessing

- Limit
- If South, West or North can go Mah-Jong with the first discard made by East, he or she scores a limit
- Calling: not applicable.

Twofold fortune

- Limit
- If a player completes a kong, draws a loose tile that completes another kong, then draws a loose tile with which he or she can go Mah-Jong, that player scores a limit
- Calling: not applicable.

Gathering the plum blossom from the roof

- Limit
- To complete this hand a player must be fishing for 5 Circles (the plum blossom). If, after picking up one of the two loose tiles from the wall as a replacement for a kong/Flower/Season, it is the 5 Circles tile and the player can go Mah-Jong, he or she scores a limit.
- Calling: not applicable.

Plucking the moon from the bottom of the sea

- Limit
- To complete this hand, a player must be fishing for the 1 Circles (the moon). If, on drawing the last tile from the wall, the player finds it is the 1 Circles and he or she can go Mah-Jong, the player scores a limit
- Calling: not applicable.

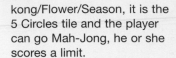

Memorising these hands makes sense, as referring to the book may give the game away.

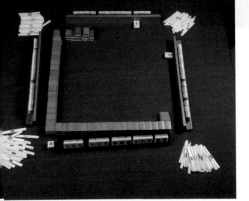

Heaven's blessing

- Limit
- If East Wind's original 14 dealt tiles give a complete hand, he or she scores a limit
- Calling: not applicable.

Heaven's blessing.

Earth's blessing.

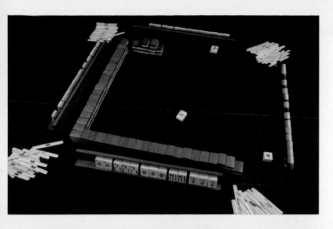

Twofold fortune.

Gathering the plum blossom from the roof.

PENALTIES

Players should keep a close eye on their own hand to ensure that they have the correct number of tiles and do not claim or discard wrongly.

INCORRECT HANDS

If players find they have too few tiles in their hand, they may not correct the error or go Mah-Jong. They may, however, count their score if another player goes out. They may not claim a discard for a pung or chow if it leaves them with no tile to discard.

If players find that they have too many tiles, they may not correct the error, go Mah-Jong or count their score.

FALSE NAMING OF DISCARDS

Any player falsely naming a discard that is claimed for a chow, pung or kong pays the other player(s) 50 points. If the false discard is claimed by another player for Mah-Jong and the tile taken is the winning piece, play stops immediately. The discarder must then pay the person claiming Mah-Jong his or her full score and settle the other players' debts to the winner. No other settlements between players take place.

FALSE DECLARATION OF MAH-JONG

When a player makes a false declaration of Mah-Jong, as long as no other players have exposed their hands, play may continue with no penalty to the mistaken player. However, should any other players expose their hand in order to count their score after a false declaration, the erring player must pay the three others points equal to a half limit score.

INCORRECT CALL

Players wrongly claiming a discard for pung, kong or chow must correct their mistake before the next player has made a discard. If the erring player fails to correct the

Players should agree at the start of the game whether penalties will be imposed – thus concentrating the mind.

mistake, the erroneously declared set remains on the table and the player, although allowed to continue in the play, may not go Mah-Jong.

LETTING OFF A CANNON

The worst crime in the game gives Mah-Jong to a player who has declared that he or she is 'fishing', and has exposed on the table any of five groups of tiles (see below) which reveal that he or she is waiting for one particular tile.

If a player lets off a cannon by discarding this tile, thereby giving Mah-Jong to an opponent, his or her penalty is to reimburse the other two players with the amount they had to pay the winner, as well as settling his or her own debt with the winner. There is then no further settlement between players.

CHOWS IN COMPANY

Chows are an essential part of the rough and ready Chinese gambling game, but are frowned upon in genteel Western play. Try to avoid them.

Players must be vigilant in discarding when any of the following groups of tiles are exposed in front of a 'fishing' player.

1. Nine tiles of the same suit: no player may discard any tile of that same suit.

2. Three pungs of Winds: no player may discard a tile of the fourth Wind – the 'fishing' player could be hoping for the special hand 'Four blessings hovering over the door' (see page 46).

3. Two pungs of Dragons: no player may discard a tile of the third Dragon – the 'fishing' player could be hoping for the special hand 'Three great scholars' (see page 46).

4. Three pungs of 1s and/or 9s: no player may discard any other 1 or 9 – the 'fishing' player could be hoping for 'Heads and tails' (see page 41).

5. Three pungs of green Bamboos and/or Green Dragons: no player may discard any other 'green' tile – the 'fishing' player could be hoping for 'Imperial jade' (see page 45).

TACTICS AND ETIQUETTE

Newcomers to Mah-Jong may be forgiven for believing that the game has nothing to do with skill, until they see how regularly experienced players win.

LUCK OR SKILL?

Luck seems to be the main feature of the game for beginners, but with expertise comes the recognition of what can be done with a hand and how to make the tiles work in one's favour.

ADAPTABILITY

Be prepared to change one's hand as circumstances dictate. For example, if one player lays out a pung of 9 Circles, 'The gates of heaven' becomes unattainable and a player trying for it must immediately change his tactics while remaining totally impassive. Through experience, players will learn alternatives when a hand becomes unattainable.

CHANGES THROUGH A GAME

For a player seeking alternatives for a special hand; by the middle of a game the chances of picking the four Winds from the wall in order to make 'The wriggling snake' have lessened considerably and the player may have discarded several tiles needed for a 'Buried treasure', whereas the odds on getting a

'Purity' hand have increased slightly. Towards the end of the game, the player needs to play a spoiling game, discarding sets of tiles to prevent anyone else going Mah-Jong.

AVOID TEMPTATION

There is always a great temptation to blindly pursue a special hand or to collect only major tiles but, time and again, players taking a quieter, less ambitious route will see their score mount slowly and surely.

To play safe from the start, collect an ordinary suit with emphasis on the sets that allow doubles (see page 33).

RACK ARRANGEMENT

Vary the arrangement of tiles in the rack because other players will soon recognise one's method of organising them. Keep as much hidden in the hand as possible - concealed sets score higher, as well as preventing the opposition knowing one's intentions.

DEFENSIVE PLAY

Players who are dealt a disastrous hand should attempt to play for a 'wash-out' (see page 26), both by discarding their single honour tiles early and by keeping a close eye on the other players' exposed sets.

OFFENSIVE PLAY

Play to win and go out as quickly as possible, claiming any discards you are allowed. Eight or more of the required tiles for any of the special hands should be held at the start of play.

Players who find no dominant suit to collect may find two or three suits of equal length which could lead to a 'Knitting' or 'Triple knitting' hand, worth a half limit.

GENERAL TACTICS
- Speed of play
- Impression of confidence
- Memorise the discards
- Collect a single suit
- Remember the doubling combinations
- Change your strategy frequently

ETIQUETTE

Certain niceties are observed. At the beginning of the game North and South should continue to wash (shuffle) the tiles until East calls 'Pow!'.

An exposed pung is always placed face up in front of a player. An exposed kong has three tiles face up and one end piece face down. A concealed pung, when displayed for scoring, must have the centre tile face down, and for a concealed kong, both end tiles are placed face down.

As soon as any player needs only one tile to go out, that player must declare to the others that he or she is 'one for Mah-Jong'.

▲ Successfully Plucking the moon from the bottom of the sea to go Mah-Jong.

BRITISH TOURNAMENT AND OTHER RULES

There are many different sets of rules for playing Mah-Jong. There are different rules for tournaments and standard games, as well as national differences.

TOURNAMENT RULES

In Mah-Jong tournaments, a number of rules differ from the standard game. The following rules reduce the element of luck that is present in the standard game:

- Only the four-handed game can be played.

- The Flowers and Seasons are not used.

- There is no 'goulash', therefore jokers are not used. If a hand ends without a player going Mah-Jong, the tiles are shuffled and dealt again without East Wind moving on.

- No player can score more than 1,000 points in one hand, except East Wind who can score 2,000 (i.e. in tournaments the limit is fixed at 1,000 points).

- No player may go Mah-Jong three times in a row with the same special hand.

THE BMJA AND OTHER RULES

As mentioned in the introduction (page 5), one of the major considerations in the creation of this book was to formalise and establish a common set of rules that could be used by all players. The success of the book over the past 30 years, with over half a million copies sold, has ensured that the BMJA rules are arguably the most widely used in the Western world. Because the game is far more popular in the East than in the West, there is still a great variety of local Eastern rules. These are some of the most common variants:

- Riichi
- MCR/OEMC
- Singapore
- Tonpuusou
- Japanese
- Zung Jung
- Dora
- World Series
- American NMJL
- American AMJA
- International Tournament

NATIONAL DIFFERENCES

Here are some ways the BMJA rules differ from play in other countries:

Chinese gambling game
In BMJA rules, a few more 'special hands' are included (see pages 38–49), and only one chow is allowed per hand.

American play
There are fewer limit hands and no insistence on 'cleared hand' play (i.e. refusing to allow a player with more than one suit in their hand to go Mah-Jong).

Japanese 'sudden death' rules
There is no need to be the first to go Mah-Jong at any cost.

JAPANESE MAH-JONG

In Japan, only the player who goes out first may be paid, which results in players going out with three chows and a pung within five moves for a score of only 22. This affords no opportunity for strategic planning through the length of a close game.

If you are planning to play Mah-Jong in China or Japan, establish which rules are being followed and leave your wallet at home!

Mah-Jong players in Fujian, China.

MAH-JONG TODAY

Today, after a long, fallow period from the 1930s to the late 1970s, Mah-Jong is gaining world interest again. The USA's National Mah-Jong League currently claims over 275,000 members, and Europe, Austria, Denmark, France, Germany, Hungary, Italy and the Netherlands all have thriving Mah-Jong communities.

INTERNATIONAL COMPETITIONS

There are 24 major international Mah-Jong tournaments held across Europe every year. The first Open European Mah-Jong Championship was held in the Netherlands, in 2005. The first World Championship in Mah-Jong was held in Tokyo, in 2002, using the standard International Tournament Rules created in China (the China State Sports Commission officially recognises Mah-Jong as a sport). The Second World Championship is hosted by Beijing in 2009.

MAH-JONG MUSEUMS

There are two Mah-Jong museums – a virtual one on the Internet, created in 1996 by American James May, and a physical one in Japan.

MANGA COMICS

Manga is the name of the Japanese comic culture. *Akagi* is a Mah-Jong manga written by Nobuyuki Fukumoto. It first appeared in 1992 in the weekly magazine *Modern Mahjong*, and was made into an animated TV series in 2005, directed by Yuzo Sato.

MOVIES

Many Western movies feature Mah-Jong games. *The Seventh Seal* and *The Thomas Crown Affair* have memorable chess set pieces, but perhaps only poker can rival Mah-Jong as the inspiration for so many films. Real film buffs acknowledge the Mah-Jong Movie as a genre in its own right, generally pushed out on a visibly low budget from Hong Kong film studios. Recent offerings include:

Kung Fu Mah-Jong (Director Wong Jing, 2005);

Fat Choi Spirit (Directors Johnnie To and Wai Ka-Fai, 2002);

Mah-Jong Dragon (Directors Jeff Lau Chun-Wai, Corey Yuen Kwai, David Lai Dai-Wai, 1997);

Mah-Jong Heroes (Director Lee Pooi-Kuen, 1981);

Ang Lee's highly regarded *Lust, Caution (*2007) opens with a frenetic game of Mah-Jong.

COLLECTING ANTIQUE SETS

There are two remarkable things about collecting Mah-Jong sets: first, their variety, and second, how cheap they are considering the craftsmanship that went into making them – the bone and ivory sets are all hand-carved and painted. Sadly their relative abundance means that there is not much of a collectors' market. Sets from the 1920s, when the popularity of the game was at its peak, are unlikely to appreciate significantly in value. On the other hand, they will never depreciate. Chinese sets (without Arabic numerals on the tiles) are more sought after than Western sets but are trickier to play with until the Chinese ideographs are mastered.

Ticket and brochure for the Mah-Jong Museum in Japan.

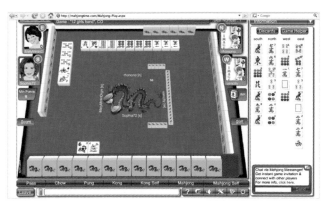
An interactive online Mah-Jong game.

MAH-JONG ONLINE

The word amateur is too often used disparagingly. To us it is the highest compliment, meaning a lover of a subject irrespective of the profit motive. There are a number of Mah-Jong Internet sites worth browsing, and the best – perhaps not the slickest, but the most content-rich – are of course run by amateurs.

UK websites
www.bmja.org.uk – closely linked to the contents of this book
www.4windsmj.com/features04.htm
www.amja.net/index.htm
www.comptechlib.com/4311.html
www.jaegerstudio.com/mjlibrary.htm
www.mahjonged.com/mahjong_rules.html
http://mahjong-europe.org
www.mahjongmuseum.com/
www.mahjongnews.com/ecriichi.htm
www.mah-jong-shop.com/index_gb.html
www.mahjongtiles.com/
www.nationalmahjongleague.org/
www.world-series-mahjong.com/

Websites in other languages
www.mahjongmuseum.nl/
historie/tweedebloei.htm
http://museum.takeshobo.co.jp/
http://uk.mahjong.dk/links/world/

INTERNET AND ARCADE GAMES

The computer/Internet game called Mah-Jong has little to do with the actual game apart from using the same tile designs. It is a form of solitaire. Arcade Mah-Jong games can be found all over Japan.

MERCHANDISE

There's a whole underworld out there providing those essential accessories that no Mah-Jong player can live without. Here is just a small selection of recent offerings:

- boxer shorts
- bracelets
- caps
- card cases
- chequebook covers
- chocolates
- clocks
- coasters
- compact mirrors
- eyeglass necklaces
- greetings cards
- guest towels
- magnets
- magnifying glasses
- mobile phone straps
- nail painting
- pretzels
- socks
- tote bags
- umbrellas
- and even a small Mah-Jong 'crying towel' for when you lose…

EPILEPSY

In 2007, the BBC reported that a study by doctors in Hong Kong concluded that epilepsy can be induced by Mah-Jong. The findings, published by four doctors from the Queen Mary Hospital in the Hong Kong Medical Journal, were based on 23 cases of people who suffered Mah-Jong-induced seizures.
The study led the writers to define Mah-Jong epilepsy as a unique syndrome. The BBC went on to comment that: "Mah-Jong is cognitively demanding, drawing on memory, fast calculations, concentration, reasoning and sequencing." The doctors concluded that the syndrome affects more men than women; that their average age is 54; and that it can hit sufferers anywhere between one to 11 hours into a Mah-Jong game.

Examples of Mah-Jong merchandise.

DOUBLING TABLE

	4	6	8	10	12	14	16
1	8	12	16	20	24	28	32
2	16	24	32	40	48	56	64
3	32	48	64	80	96	112	128
4	64	96	128	160	192	224	256
5	128	192	256	320	384	448	512
6	256	384	512	640	768	896	**1024**

	32	34	36	38	40	42	44
1	63	68	72	76	80	84	88
2	128	136	144	152	160	168	176
3	256	272	288	304	320	336	352
4	512	544	576	608	640	672	704
5	**1024**	**1088**	**1152**	**1216**	**1280**	**1344**	**1408**
6	**2048**	**2176**	**2304**	**2432**	**2560**	**2688**	**2816**

	60	62	64	66	68	70	72
1	120	124	128	132	136	140	144
2	240	248	256	264	272	280	288
3	380	496	512	528	544	560	576
4	960	992	**1024**	**1056**	**1088**	**1120**	**1152**
5	**1920**	**1948**	**2048**	**2112**	**2176**	**2240**	**2304**
6	**3840**	**3968**	**4096**	**4224**	**4352**	**4480**	**4608**

	88	90	92	94	96	98	100
1	176	180	184	188	192	196	200
2	352	360	368	376	384	392	400
3	704	720	736	752	768	784	800
4	**1408**	**1440**	**1472**	**1504**	**1536**	**1568**	**1600**
5	**2816**	**2880**	**2944**	**3008**	**3072**	**3136**	**3200**
6	**5632**	**5760**	**5888**	**6016**	**6144**	**6272**	**6400**

18	20	22	24	26	28	30
36	40	44	48	52	56	60
72	80	88	96	104	112	120
144	160	176	192	208	224	240
288	320	352	384	416	448	480
576	640	704	768	832	896	960
1152	**1280**	**1408**	**1536**	**1664**	**1792**	**1920**

46	48	50	52	54	56	58
92	96	100	104	108	112	116
184	192	200	208	216	224	232
368	384	400	416	432	448	464
736	768	800	832	864	896	928
1472	**1536**	**1600**	**1664**	**1728**	**1792**	**1856**
2944	**3072**	**3200**	**3328**	**3456**	**3584**	**3712**

74	76	78	80	82	84	86
148	152	156	160	164	168	172
296	304	312	320	328	336	344
592	608	624	640	656	672	688
1184	**1216**	**1248**	**1280**	**1312**	**1344**	**1376**
2368	**2432**	**2496**	**2560**	**2624**	**2688**	**2752**
4736	**4864**	**4992**	**5120**	**5248**	**5376**	**5504**

**In tournament play, all scores in bold
count as 1,000 points only.**

GLOSSARY

Bouquet A set of all four Flowers or Seasons (not a mixture of both) held by one player (also known as a complete set).

Calling/calling hand Being 'one for Mah-Jong'; needing one more tile to complete a hand. Also called 'fishing'.

Chow A run of three tiles in the same suit – 3, 4, 5 Circles.

Completed hand One with which a player has gone Mah-Jong.

Concealed A pung, chow or kong collected in the hand with tiles from the wall rather than from discards. A special hand may also be concealed until the player goes out.

Dead tiles All the unclaimed discards; these have no further role in the game.

Declare A player needing one more tile to go out must declare that he is 'one for Mah-Jong'.

Discard To place an unwanted tile face up on the table in the middle of the playing area. Players must discard a tile at each turn, unless they are going Mah-Jong.

Exposed A pung, chow or kong claimed from another player's discard and displayed on the table in front of him.

False declaration/discard Falsely declaring that one has gone Mah-Jong or naming a discard claimed by another player. Penalties may apply.

Goulash This comes into play if no one goes Mah-Jong. Jokers are used to replace the 2 Bamboos and each player exchanges three tiles with each of the other three players before continuing the hand.

Half limit The limit is usually 1,000 points – a half limit (500) is the score awarded for some special hands.

Jokers The four tiles used in a goulash to replace the 2 Bamboos; they are 'wild'.

Kong A set of four identical tiles – four 9 Characters.

Kong box The 14 tiles separated from the rest of the wall from which replacement tiles for Flowers, Seasons and kongs are taken. The kong box is not replenished during play. Also known as the 'dead wall'.

Letting off a cannon Discarding a tile that another player who has declared he is 'fishing' is almost certainly waiting for, and which enables him to go Mah-Jong. Penalties will apply.

Limit/limit hand Usually 1,000. Agreed by the players, this is the highest score anyone can make for a single hand after Mah-Jong has been declared.

Loose tiles Taken from the end of the kong box closest to where the wall was broken and placed on the top. As loose tiles are claimed, the next pair is placed on top of the kong box until none of the 14 tiles remains.

Mah-Jong, One for To need only one more tile to complete one's hand and go out (go Mah-Jong).

Mah-Jong, To go Complete one's hand and go out.

Original call A hand which, after the first discard, has become a calling hand. The player must declare an 'original call' at once.

Pow The call made by East to tell the other players to stop shuffling the tiles and build the wall.

Prevailing wind Also called the wind of the round; this is always East in the first round, then South, followed by West and lastly North.

Robbing the kong A move in which a player takes a tile from an opponent's exposed kong and immediately goes Mah-Jong.

Run A series of consecutively numbered tiles of the same suit. Three make up a chow.

Sets Sets of tiles are called pungs, chows and kongs. A Mah-jong set comprises all the playing pieces, jokers, Flowers and Seasons, dice and tallies, plus wind discs, tong box and plain replacement tiles.

Settling up The payment in tallies after each hand is completed.

Special hands There are nineteen special hands that are worth set scores if achieved – limit or half limit. Many are collected concealed in the hand.

Suit Three sets or suits of tiles: Bamboos, Characters and Circles.

Winning tile The final tile needed to complete a hand and enable the player to go Mah-Jong.

INDEX